Completing a Child's Permanence Report

A guide to collecting and analysing information for a Child's Permanence Report (CPR) (England)

Elaine Dibben with Lyn Bugarski, Nicky Probert and Julia Wilson

www.baaf.org.uk

Published by

British Association for Adoption & Fostering

(BAAF)

Saffron House

6–10 Kirby Street

London EC1N 8TS

www.baaf.org.uk

Charity registration 275689 (England and Wales) and SC039337 (Scotland)

© BAAF, 2014

British Library Cataloguing in Publication Data

A catalogue record for this book is available from the British Library

ISBN 978 1 910039 17 5

Project management by Jo Francis, Publications Department, BAAF

Designed by Helen Joubert Designs

Printed in Great Britain by The Lavenham Press

BAAF is the leading UK-wide membership organisation for all those concerned with adoption, fostering and child care issues.

Contents

Acknowledgements

This book has been written to accompany the BAAF form CPR which was published in May 2014. In addition to the contributions of the co-authors, who have all been passionate about the importance of raising the quality of CPRs, this book has benefited from discussions held with the managers who took the lead in their agencies piloting the CPR between September 2013 and March 2014, and who shared their views on what social workers needed to know and think about when completing a CPR. I would particularly like to thank Peter Hodgkinson from Plymouth City Council and Sue Clarke from Calderdale MBC for reading and sharing their comments on this book from the perspective of agencies that are using the form.

I would also like to thank Bernard Monaghan, who offered his insights as an adoption panel Chair; Lorraine Pearson, who brought her perspective as a medical adviser; Florence Merredew, for looking at aspects of child health; Julia Feast, who devised Appendix H; and Helen Maybee, for sharing the CPR Checklist, which is used in Dudley MBC and which I have adapted and included as an appendix to this book.

Finally, my thanks to Harina Patel for all her administrative support in bringing this book to fruition, and to Shaila Shah and Jo Francis in BAAF Publications for their support and encouragement.

Notes about the authors

Elaine Dibben started her social work career in residential social work and qualified in 1988. She has over 25 years' experience of working in adoption and fostering in local authority and voluntary adoption agency settings. She joined BAAF in 2004 to become manager of the Independent Review Mechanism, which she set up and ran until 2009, when she moved to take on a wider role in BAAF as a trainer/consultant. She is currently an Adoption Development Consultant for BAAF, alongside acting as a Panel Chair for both adoption and fostering panels.

She has written several good practice guides, published by BAAF – *Devising a Placement Plan* (2012), *Parent and Child Fostering*, with Paul Adams (2011), *Preparing to Adopt* (2014) with Eileen Fursland and Nicky Probert, and *Undertaking an Adoption Assessment in England* (2010) (second edition 2013).

She lives in Oxfordshire with her husband, Steve.

Lyn Bugarski qualified as a social worker in 1982 and has worked in fostering and adoption since 1985, primarily in local authority settings. She currently works as the Professional Adviser on Adoption for Derby City Council and also undertakes some independent work. Lyn believes it is important to consider the lifelong implications of adoption and to learn from the messages given by adopted people. She is also committed to developing adoption support services.

Lyn has two adult daughters and lives in Derbyshire.

Nicky Probert gained a Master's degree in Social Work and qualified as a social worker in 1985 after working with children and young people in residential care and the youth justice system. She then worked with family placement services. On moving to the Midlands, Nicky worked directly with children and young people, doing life story work and post-abuse counselling and conducting risk assessments with families.

Nicky has been working in family placements for over 25 years and in 2003, she joined BAAF to help disseminate and share best practice with colleagues involved in social care.

Nicky has two adult children from her first marriage and currently lives in Birmingham with her partner and his daughter.

Julia Wilson qualified as a social worker in 1979. During the last 32 years, she has worked for a number of local authorities and a voluntary organisation specialising in fostering and adoption, both at practitioner and managerial level. More recently, she has been the Professional Adviser for the Adoption Panels for a local authority in the Midlands, a role that has included quality-assuring Child's Permanence Reports and other documentation before the agency decision-maker considers a plan for adoption.

In 1991, Julia and her husband adopted a sibling group of three children aged 10, eight and four.

How to use this guide

Introduction

The Child's Permanence Report (CPR) is one of the most important reports that a social worker will be asked to complete. It provides information that will be the basis of how the child understands their history during their childhood and throughout their adult life. The significance of this report can be seen by the fact that the CPR is one of the primary documents that has to be kept securely, as part of an adoption case record, for 100 years after an adoption order is made. It is also designed to be the primary document used to enable the agency decision-maker (ADM) to reach their decision that the child "should be placed for adoption". Where a child is being placed for adoption with the consent of their birth parents, the CPR will also provide the adoption panel with information to reach their recommendation about the child being placed for adoption.

When completing this report, it is important to remember its different functions, purposes and potential audiences.

- The agency decision-maker, CAFCASS guardians, judges during the court process and adoption panel members will make life-changing decisions for the child and their family based on information in this report.

- Family-finding social workers, along with prospective adoptive parents, will be greatly influenced by the report during linking and matching in deciding whether they can meet the needs of this child. For adopters, this will often include a sense of "chemistry" or shared talents and interests when reading about the child, so it is really important that the report "brings the child to life".

- Finally, the adopted child/adult will gain an understanding, from the information in the report, of the life experiences that have shaped them and the reasons why they were adopted, and will be seeking to understand "their story".

The 2014 version of the CPR has been designed so that, following the agency decision, the report can be used as the Annex B report to accompany the placement order application. Chapter 8 of the 2013 Adoption Statutory Guidance (SG) 8.82 noted that 'There is also considerable similarity between the information required in both reports', and stated, 'To reduce delay, local authorities should consider how to enable information contained in the local authority's electronic recording system to be transferred into a format acceptable to the court and complying with the requirements of Rule 14.11 and the Practice Direction, to eliminate duplication of work for social workers.'

Whilst BAAF is aware that some individual agencies have designed formats to meet the requirements of the Adoption Agencies Regulations (AAR) 2005 as well as the Family Procedure Rules 2010 (FPR) (Practice Direction 14C, Annex B), it was felt that there would be benefits in offering a form that could be used by all local authorities in England, to ensure consistency.

The provision of the CPR as a decision-making tool and the required contents are set out in AAR 17 and in SG 2014 Chapter 1, which states that:

- *The CPR must include all the information about the child and their family and a summary by the agency's medical adviser.*

- *The accuracy of the CPR is essential, since it will not only form the basis on which decisions are made about whether the child should be placed for adoption but will also assist the agency in matching the child with an appropriate prospective adopter. The CPR will be the source of the information about the child on which the prospective adopter will rely. The child, on reaching adulthood, will be able to request a copy of the CPR under the AIR (the Adoption Information and Intermediary Services (Pre-Commencement Adoptions) Regulations 2005) and may have to rely on this document as the principal source of information about their pre-adoption history.*

(Statutory Adoption Guidance, 2014)

Although this guide has been designed to accompany the CPR (England), it may be helpful for social workers in other parts of the UK.

Who should complete the CPR?

Chapter 1 in the Adoption Statutory Guidance states that:

...the social worker who knows the child best should compile the CPR provided they meet the requirements of the Restriction on the Preparation of Adoption Reports Regulations 2005 (ARR).

These regulations state that the CPR must be completed by a social worker with at least three years' post-qualifying experience in child care social work, including direct experience of adoption work, or be supervised by a social worker who is employed by the local authority and has at least three years' post-qualifying experience in child care social work, including direct experience of adoption work. Where the child's social worker does not meet the requirements, it will be important that adequate supervision is provided to them during the writing of the report and that it is read thoroughly before being signed off by the supervisor. It can be helpful to look at other completed CPRs that have been commended by the adoption panel or decision-maker, but it is not appropriate to "copy and paste" text from other reports.

Confidentiality

Section 60(2)(b) of the Adoption and Children Act 2002 (ACA) provides for an adopted person, at 18, to receive from the appropriate adoption agency (AAA) the information disclosed under section 54 of the ACA 2002 to the prospective adopters during the adoption process. This includes the CPR, which will:

...include identifying information about the child, the birth parents, birth siblings and possibly other members of the birth family. It will also include information about the child's early life and family history, their social, emotional and behavioural development and other matters.

Although information contained in the CPR does not require consent to be given by the people referred to, SG Chapter 1 sets out the following expectations:

- *It is important therefore that the information contained in the CPR is checked against the original sources of information. Those parts of the CPR that contain factual information about the birth family should be shared with the relevant family members to enable them to confirm their accuracy and agree to it being passed on to the child in due course. Any such agreement should be clearly recorded on the child's case record.*

- *Each of the child's parents should also be shown those parts of the CPR which set out their views and wishes, and given the opportunity, if they so wish, to express these in their own words. Where writing is not their preferred means of communication, they could be assisted to express their wishes by other means such as an audio-recording. Where the child is old enough, they should also be encouraged to confirm that their views have been accurately stated. The CPR should make it clear whether the parents have seen the CPR, or parts of it, and include any comments they have expressed on it.*

It is important, therefore, that where birth parents or other relatives do not agree with any of the information, this is stated in the CPR.

Social workers must also be aware that any additional information held on the child's file, which is deemed to be "identifying information" and is not included in the CPR, will be subject to the requirements of the Disclosure of Adoption Information (Post-Commencement Adoptions) Regulations 2005 as section 56 information, which requires the consent of those people to whom the information refers in order for the AAA to share information with the adopted adult. Therefore, it would be an advantage for future working if the consents were gained from those relatives at the time of completing the CPR, in case the child, once they are an adult, requires additional information. A template for this is included in Appendix G.

Where the CPR is being used as the Annex B report, Chapter 5(7) in the Statutory Guidance on Court Orders and Pre-proceedings April 2014 (SGCO) sets out:

Although the report is confidential, parts of it are likely to be shared with the parties to the proceedings. In a case where the prospective adopter's identity is not to be disclosed to the birth parents, care must be taken to ensure that any identifying information is contained in a separate section which is not to be disclosed except to

*the court and any Children's Guardian or family court reporter. Identifying
information may include addresses, employment and, for example, the name of the
school attended by the child.*

This separate section could also include the name and address of the current foster carer,
particularly where the care plan is for that carer to adopt the child or where this is a
Fostering for Adoption placement.

A brief overview of the Child's Permanence Report

The headings of the CPR have been ordered as much as possible to meet the
requirements of both the Annex B report and the Adoption Agencies Regulations,
including Schedule 1, whilst maintaining the coherence of the child's story.

Part 1 starts by setting out details of workers involved with the child, essential
information about the child and their birth family, their legal status, and a chronology of
their care. It then provides detailed information about the child, their health and
education, their history, including their family history where it impacts on the child, and
an analysis of their needs, wishes and feelings and detailed information about the child's
birth parents and siblings.

Part 2 covers the current and future contact arrangements for the child and their birth
family and any other significant people.

Part 3 provides a summary of the actions of the local authority, including counselling and
ascertaining the views of the birth parents, decision-making about the ability of others to
care for the child, and the final recommendations and reasoning behind them.

The guidance notes and additional resources are designed to provide support to
the social worker writing the report. They comprise a checklist that can be included with
the CPR as needed, the guidance notes referenced in the report, and forms that can be
used with birth parents and the child to obtain their views and inform the relevant
sections of the CPR.

How to use this guide

It is hoped that, by making use of this guide, child care social workers writing these
reports will be able to think about how to collect the information needed from a variety of
sources during their involvement with the child. Some information may well be more
easily provided early in the local authority's involvement with birth family members, who
may later become less involved, cease all contact with social workers, or become more
reluctant to share information once adoption becomes the local authority plan.

This means that social workers need to be aware that as soon as adoption becomes a possible permanent option for the child, they must start to gather personal information from the birth parents or others who will be important to the child in the future.

Information can be provided by birth parents and extended family members, nursery and/or school teachers, previous and current foster carers, therapists, and from psychologists' reports. It is important that the views of people who know the child in different settings are included to give a rounded picture of the child and for the social worker to then provide analysis of the information, particularly where different pictures of the child are being presented. Details of where the information has been sourced should be included in the child's adoption file, as well as being highlighted in the CPR.

This guide looks at all sections of the CPR and provides extracts from relevant statutory guidance or from the guidance notes that accompany the CPR, and a list of questions or areas that need to be covered, as well as tips to ensure that the report is well drafted.

This guide is not intended to be a quick and easy way of undertaking the CPR. It assumes that the social worker will review the child's file to ensure that any information obtained prior to their involvement is not missed; arrange for external reports such as health reports and school reports to be available to the social worker at the time of writing the report; and ensure that all relevant people have been spoken to.

Although the guide poses a list of questions to the social worker, it is recognised that to obtain full information on what may be sensitive issues, the worker may need several attempts to obtain personal information from the child's birth parents, and may need to use other sources, such as extended family members or information provided to other professionals during assessments undertaken with them. It may be that another professional, such as the social worker providing independent counselling or a support worker tasked to undertake life story work, may gain more co-operation from the birth parents when obtaining personal information.

Part 1: Information about the child

Family tree/genogram

The completion of a family tree/genogram is a requirement of the AAR 2005 Regulation 15(1) Schedule 1.19, which sets out the need for 'so far as is possible, a family tree with details of the child's grandparents, parents and aunts and uncles with their age (or ages at death)'.

> **The child's family tree is required by the AAR. The template for the genogram in the care application can be used here, updated if needed. Where a family is very large and/or complicated, it may be clearer to list the relevant family members in the family composition section. The genogram should normally go back to the child's grandparents' generation and include all siblings and half-siblings, and significant extended family members. Use dates of birth where known rather than ages.**
>
> **Guidance notes to CPR**

The family tree/genogram provides a pictorial representation of the child's extended family and may be a helpful tool to understand complex family relationships/structures. It is important at the time of writing to include all known children, including half-siblings and those adopted out of the family as well as any as yet unborn child.

It is helpful to involve birth parents in producing the family tree/genogram, to ensure that all family members are included. The family tree/genogram will prove an important addition to a child's life story book – the information is not just for the child in the present, but for the child in later life, who may well need to know names of aunts, uncles and cousins if they want to re-establish contact with their birth family.

Where family trees have been completed at an earlier point in the local authority's involvement with the family, ensure that these are correct and up to date.

Examples of both a family tree/genogram and a family structure are provided in Appendix A.

Legal status of the child

This information is required by both the AAR and the FPR. The information will need to be updated at the point of a match being made.

CAFCASS Guardian's views

> **Where court proceedings are taking place, it is important that the Children's Guardian's views are conveyed to the decision-maker, particularly if these differ from those of the local authority. Their view at this stage will be a provisional one based on the evidence available and it should be made clear whether they have provided a written view which has been inserted into the report or whether the social worker is representing their view given verbally.**
>
> **There may also be expert reports available which have been prepared in connection with the court proceedings. Although this may sometimes give rise to difficulties of timing, it is essential that these or a summary (agreed between the local authority's legal adviser and the other parties to the proceedings) should be made available to the decision-maker.**
>
> **Guidance notes to CPR**

The requirement for the Guardian's view is set out in SG 1.50.

> *Where court proceedings are taking place, it is important that the Children's Guardian's views are conveyed to the decision-maker, particularly if these differ from those of the local authority.*

It is also set out in case law – *Re R (Adoption Disclosure) [1999]* – where it was stated that:

> *... the regulations required the adoption agency to give the panel a written report containing 'any information relevant', and such information must include the views of other professionals who had been involved in considering the future of the children. Therefore an adoption agency should state the views of the guardian ad litem, if then known, within its written report to the panel. Further, if the guardian had not by then formulated any final views, the panel should be informed of this negative fact as part of the relevant information.*

At the time when the CPR is being written, it is likely that the Guardian may not have seen all the final reports for court or submitted their report. The social worker is therefore likely to be asking the Guardian for a preliminary view based on the information available at that point, and will therefore need to update this section at the time of matching. If the social worker is only able to obtain a verbal view from the Guardian, they must ensure that what is then written in the CPR is shown to the Guardian for their agreement, to ensure that the principles set out in *Re B [2008]* are adhered to.

A proforma to obtain the Guardian's view is included in Appendix B.

Chronology

> ## Chronology of the child's care since birth
>
> The chronology should include all of the moves and changes of carer experienced by the child to date, including parents and other birth family members as well as other carers. The Annex B requires observations on the care provided in each placement. This should be a brief overall summary as it can be covered in more detail as needed in the child's history. The placement details should describe the type of placement (e.g. with family members, foster placement, residential, etc), who the carers were, and state briefly the reasons for any move/change of placement, with more detail being provided in the child's history section.
>
> **Guidance notes to CPR**

This chronology is required by the AAR and FPR and it is important that it sets out all the placements and moves experienced by the child. This would include moves made between birth parents or other extended family members, which may have occurred before the child came into care. It should also include periods of respite foster placements made after the child came into foster care and any periods of residential assessment with their birth parents. An example of a chronology of care is included in Appendix C.

Description of the child

> **The physical description should complement the photograph of the child and should include any information not obvious in the photograph, for example, if the child is bigger or smaller than the average for his or her age and any striking characteristics.**
>
> **Guidance notes to CPR**

The description of the child should complement the photograph featured on the front page of the report. It is important that the photograph is as up to date as possible as this will be a significant feature of the report when seen by prospective adopters. The date that the photograph was taken should also be recorded.

You should include the following details:

- Colour and length of hair
- Colour of eyes
- Skin tone/colouring
- The child's stature – whether small or big for his/her age
- Any physical characteristics such as scars, a squint, a cleft palate, etc
- Include the type of physical features that people will notice when they first meet the child, for example, does he/she wear glasses?

Personality

> **Briefly describe the child's personality. Given the subjective nature of this description and the likelihood that the child will read this in later life, considerable care should be exercised in using words and phrases that are accurate and give a balanced and helpful picture of the child. All descriptions of the child will need updating to reflect the child's development. The foster carer will often be the best placed to "bring the child to life", but it will be important for the social worker to also draw on their own knowledge of the child as well as that of other relevant people, e.g. teachers, nursery workers, parents. It should be made clear where information/views about the child have come from and if there are differing perceptions of the child in different settings.**
>
> **Guidance notes to CPR**

You could include the following suggested details, as appropriate to the child's age.

- Describe the child's temperament – is the child shy, placid, chatty, happy, friendly, withdrawn, extrovert?
- How well does he/she mix with and interact with other children?
- How curious is he/she?
- If this report is about a baby, is the child generally contented and responsive to others, etc?
- Are the child's responses within the "norms" of development for their age?
- If this report is about a young child, does the child have mechanisms to manage his/her anxiety, such as a security blanket?
- Does the child have any fears, for example, loud music, showers?

Interests, likes and dislikes

Describe the child's particular interest in hobbies, music, sporting activities, etc. If she or he has particular aptitudes or talents, these should be noted. If there are significant things the child dislikes, these should also be noted.

Guidance notes to CPR

You should include the following details.

- Does the child have any strong likes and dislikes regarding food?
- How does the child feel about or react to any pets in this family or in previous homes?
- What activities does the child enjoy, e.g. playing or watching sports, school or community-based clubs, listening to music, outdoor play, visiting places (give examples)?
- Does the child have a favourite toy, books, films, computer games?
- What are their preferred clothes; do they have favourite colours?
- Does the child like to help the carer with activities such as cooking?

This information can be helpfully cross-referenced into the child's life story book.

Self-care skills

Information on self-care should be given in relation to the child's age and developmental stage.

- **Describe the child's capacity to appropriately care for themselves in relation to their age and abilities.**

- **Describe the child's daily routines including eating, washing, toileting, getting dressed, bedtimes, leaving for playgroup/nursery/ school.**

- **Are there any specific factors that need to be taken into account in placing the child in an adoptive family? This should include any special arrangements needed to support the child in developing their self-care skills or daily routines.**

- **If the child has any particular dislikes in relation to daily routines, self-care, etc, these should be described.**

Guidance notes to CPR

It is important to ensure that information in this section takes account of the child's age and development but also recognises if the child is functioning at a level which would be expected of an older or younger child. Information from the foster carer's report, usually gained through the BAAF Form C, will help you complete this section.

You could also include the following suggested details as appropriate to the child's age.

- If this child is a baby, how far is he/she able to self-soothe?

- How much does the child depend on their carer or ask for their involvement in key areas such as eating, toileting, dressing, and washing?

- How safe is the child to play outside? Does he/she need supervision?

- If the child has specific needs regarding hair and skin care, what help does he/she need with this?

- What are the areas where the child is functioning above or below his/her age?

- Is the child resistant to help from their carer and more independent than expected for his/her age?

Emotional, behavioural and social development

The child's current level of emotional, behavioural and social development should include a description and evaluation of the child's capacity for making and sustaining relationships, and address the following:

- how their current carers describe them in terms of warmth, enjoyment or wariness of intimacy, their playfulness, their responses to daily routines, to boundaries being set and to change in routines or circumstances;

- how the child is developing relationships with other children in the family, including siblings, foster children or the birth children of their carers;

- how the child is developing relationships with those outside the family such as friends, children at school, teachers;

- do they maintain appropriate wariness of strangers or are they over-familiar?

- the child's developing "sense of belonging" to important people in their life;

- information from any strengths/difficulties questionnaire (SDQ) completed.

Guidance notes to CPR

You could also include the following suggested details as appropriate to the child's age.

- Is the child able to display a full range of emotions?

- Can the child regulate his/her emotions in an age-appropriate way, e.g. what are their triggers for temper tantrums and in what settings do these occur?

- Does the child have any unusual behaviours?

- Are there things that are concerning/indicate issues, e.g. disturbed sleep patterns?

- What attachments has the child formed?

- How does the child relate to adults, other than his/her main carers?

- Are there differences in how the child relates to men and women – in the foster home and other settings?

- What situations does the child find most difficult to cope with?

Identity

Under identity, consider the child's awareness of his or her relationship to the birth family and foster family and the development of their identity.

Each child will have a developing sense of who they are and what is important in the world around them. This will become the basis of self-esteem and identity.

There are a number of factors that build towards this: the child's physical capacities, including any disability, their social class, culture, their ethnicity, their language, their religion, their gender, their sexuality. Each of these factors singly and in combination will influence the way the child feels, thinks, behaves and makes relationships.

It will be central to their sense of belonging to important people and their sense of community, culture and wider society. The people who care for them and provide them with opportunities and guidance will be vital in this.

Adoption itself will have an important impact on the child's developing sense of self, including the acquisition of an "adoption identity". Include details in this section about the child's ethnicity, religion and how the child views himself/herself.

Guidance notes to CPR

You could include the following suggested details as appropriate to the child's age.

- If this is a young child, does he/she respond to and know his/her name?
- How strongly does the child identify with his/her birth parents and any siblings?
- Does the child identify himself/herself with a particular geographic area?
- Does the child identify with a particular social group, football or rugby club, scouts or guides, etc?
- Has the child been involved in any life story work or memory work? Does he/she have any photos or information to help understand their past?
- If the child is from a minority ethnic background, has any work been done with him/her on understanding his/her heritage?
- When describing ethnicity, be specific, e.g. white-Scottish/Black Caribbean – St Kitts would give a child a much clearer idea of their ethnicity and cultural heritage than white/Caribbean.

- Where there are family members from other ethnic backgrounds, give as many details as possible: which Caribbean island, caste, etc.

Religion

You should include the following details.

- Does the child actively participate in his/her religious faith?
- Has the child been formally admitted to his/her religion through a recognised ceremony (state which)?
- Are there specific needs in relation to the child's religion?
- Have the child's birth parents made any specific requests about religion for their child?
- Do the birth parents actively practise a religion?
- Be specific about the denomination of the birth parents' religion (for example, there are over 100 different Christian denominations and five main sects of Islam).
- What has the child's experience of religion been in his/her foster placement?

Language

You should include the following details.

- What was the main language used in the child's birth family?
- What is the main language used in the child's current placement?
- If English is not the child's first language, what support has he/she needed around developing his/her language?
- Are there any other languages that the child has experienced through other family members/carers?
- Are there other communication methods used by birth family members or the child, e.g. British Sign Language, Makaton, other pictorial languages?

Health

The health section should not duplicate information from the medical adviser's summary but should give information about the child's general health and mental health and any learning difficulties if these are not covered in the medical report. It can include observations from foster carers on the child's general health and give details such as their height and weight and whether they are meeting their developmental milestones.

The summary report from the agency medical adviser should be attached or inserted into the report. This must include the child's health history, current state of health and any anticipated health care needs (AAR 17b); information about the birth parents' health, including any known learning difficulties, medical or mental health factors which are likely to or may have genetic implications for the child (AAR 16(2)); and the date of the most recent medical examination. It is very important to ensure that any known genetic risk factors or any health conditions or disability which may be significant are identified here and information about the child's family health history which may be relevant to the child's future and future placement is highlighted. Where information about birth parents' health is disclosed during assessments undertaken during proceedings, the social worker should ensure this updated information is passed on to the medical adviser so the medical summary can be updated.

Guidance notes to CPR

This section should not duplicate the medical adviser's summary. However, it should include any updated information since the medical reports were prepared, for example, from court reports, psychologist's or educational psychologist's reports. See Appendix D for a list of BAAF health forms that can inform the medical adviser's report.

If there is anything known about the health of the child's birth parents or extended family members, which was not included in the original medical reports, this information should also be shared with the agency medical adviser and used to inform an update of the adoption medical. SG 1.45 sets out that the CPR must include the agency's medical adviser's summary and that detailed health reports should only be provided to the agency decision-maker or adoption panel if the medical adviser considers that this is necessary. There is an expectation that the agency should make the medical adviser aware of all medical information about the child and his/her birth family so that this can inform decision-making by the agency decision maker, courts and later, the prospective adopters.

Do not include any health information about particular conditions that has been obtained from the internet or from unqualified people unless it has been seen and agreed by the medical adviser.

You should include the following details.

- What information has been shared by the child's birth parents about their family or own health history? Clarify whether this is anecdotal or has been verified by a medical professional.

- Be aware of the genetic implications for the child's future health – if a birth parent or grandparent has died, try to identify the cause.

- What health-related issues has the child managed on a day-to-day basis? Does the child have any vulnerabilities, e.g. high or low tolerance of pain, or recurring conditions?

- Does the child have any allergies that impact upon his/her daily life, e.g. pets, food?

- Has the child had any referrals relating to his/her emotional health or received any interventions or ongoing treatment?

- Have all the previous recommendations from LAC medicals been followed up, e.g. recommendations re: Hepatitis B, HIV tests, immunisations?

- Does the child receive any specialist services for his/her overall health which are not set out elsewhere?

Education

> Using the details from the section on the child's education, outline the significant factors about the child's education (including early education in playgroups or nursery) and their progress to date, and the anticipated needs of the child in relation to their education that should be taken into account in planning the adoptive placement. If the child is of nursery or school age, include any key points or recommendations from the child's Personal Education Plan (PEP).
>
> Detail the child's experience of education. What sort of educational experiences has he or she enjoyed? Where there is some indication of the sort of educational setting which will best suit the child, give details so prospective adopters can begin to research this in their area.
>
> **Guidance notes to CPR**

You should also include the following details.

- What are the child's preferred/favourite topics or subjects at school?

- Has the child had any particular achievements in school or nursery, e.g. awards, certificates?

- Does the child undertake any additional educational activities outside school, e.g. learning an instrument (if not already stated), extra tutoring?

- What does the child struggle with in school, both academically and/or socially? How is he/she in the classroom and during unstructured play times?

- Are there any characteristics of the child's school/nursery that have been positive/ negative for the child, e.g. small village school, ethnic mix of school, size of classes?

Family history

Summary of relevant family history and the child's history

This is a crucial section and should be written specifically for this report, rather than being "cut and pasted" from other reports. A brief summary should be given of the relevant family history to help explain the local authority's involvement and the situation the child was born into. Each birth parent's history can be covered in more depth in later sections.

Guidance notes to CPR

It is important that this section should be written specifically for this report and that it provides a clear understanding of how earlier events contributed to the planning for this child. However, only a summary is required so it would usually be written in a few paragraphs. Further details of significant decisions may be included in the chronology of agency decisions so that you can refer to these rather than repeating the information.

It is important that the information given here does not include unnecessary details relating to the experiences of the child's siblings, as this could contravene data protection principles. Also, it should not include graphic details in relation to abuse of any other children.

The areas that should be covered include the following:

- Where the local authority has previously been involved with other children in the family, what were the main reasons for that involvement and what were the outcomes for the children?

- When the current involvement is based on concerns relating to previous children, how has the previous history led to the local authority's looking after this child and recommending adoption for him/her?

- What contact did the local authority or any other professionals have with the family prior to becoming involved with the child?

The child's history

The child's history section should be used to set out this child's "story" and bring together the facts contained in other parts of this report to "tell" this story. This section should therefore be both a description and an analysis, and should include the following:

- Prenatal experiences, where known. Was the child exposed to alcohol and/or other substances? Include prescription medication as well as illicit drugs. Was there domestic violence or other trauma during the mother's pregnancy? This should be based not just on parental reports, but also evidence from other sources, for example, medical or police reports.

- The structure and membership of the child's birth family, drawing on information from the family tree.

- The child's relationships with their birth mother and father and other members of the extended family who have cared for them and how these have impacted on the child.

- Their experience of being parented by their birth parents and the reasons they became looked after.

- The known facts about and consequences of any abuse or neglect, and how this has influenced the child's emotional and behavioural development.

- Include any significant events, both positive and negative, which the child may have some memory of and also identify any gaps in the child's records.

- Their experiences of being cared for by foster carers, residential care workers or others as their principal carers. Refer back to the chronology of care and expand on the reasons for any changes of carer and consider the way in which previous moves occurred and have impacted on the child's emotional and behavioural development.

- This section should cover up to the present day and will need to be updated at each point the report is used.

Guidance notes to CPR

This section should include information about the child that is not available in other sections of the report. It should capture for the reader: who the child has lived with; who their main caregivers have been to date; and the quality of care that the child has received. Ensure that this account sets out both positive and negative experiences of being parented, where possible. It should identify periods of good parenting that the child has received and also include any significant events that have influenced your recommendation, e.g. evidence of neglect and abuse, concerns about parenting capacity, and reasons for concern leading to the plan for adoption.

In the future, this information will form the basis of the child's later life letter. Bring it up to date to include experiences since the child has been in care. Point out any significant gaps in your knowledge. Do not be afraid to include positive experiences, but do not "sanitise" the story.

Update this section when the CPR is being presented to the panel as part of the matching paperwork. Remember that for a young child, particularly, information can quickly become out of date.

As well as factual information, this section should provide an analysis of the impact of the child's history on his/her future development and the child's ability to make secure attachments, e.g. the impact of several moves and several caregivers.

Analysis of the child's needs

This should be an analysis and summary of the child's needs based on their history and should include information provided from other sources, e.g. the current carer, school, health professionals. The social worker can consider the skills and qualities which a prospective adopter will need but should not be too prescriptive about the characteristics required of adopters, e.g. only able to consider a two-parent family, or stating preferred ethnicity.

Guidance notes to CPR

Based on the child's past history and current experience, highlight the child's main/significant needs in relation to the following:

- forming attachments;
- health needs;
- educational needs;
- identity needs.

Set out the implications of these needs for the child's future placement.

- Are there specific skills or experience that prospective adopters might need?
- Is there training or support that should be available to the adopters?
- What challenges might there be in helping the child understand his/her story in the future?

- Are there areas of uncertainty about the child's future development that prospective adopters should be aware of?

- Are there identified support needs for the child in the future to be aware of, e.g. therapy, sibling contact?

- Are there any geographic considerations based on keeping the child safe or services that the child will need to be able to access?

- Where others have provided information about the child and his/her needs, be aware of anything that may have "clouded" their judgment or influenced their views, e.g. a teacher who finds a child difficult to manage or a foster carer who expresses concern about placing a child with a single carer.

- Where you are recommending a specific family setting for the child, e.g. a two-parent family, make sure you have evidenced why this is needed and ensured that it will not unnecessarily limit the child's chances of placement.

The child's wishes and feelings

Information from the child's wishes and feelings worksheet, where used with children who are old enough, can be reflected here but this section should also take account of the wishes and feelings the child has expressed in other ways, for example, to foster carers, in contact sessions and at school. This section should be updated to reflect the child's changing understanding and development. Include the date when the child's wishes and feelings were last ascertained.

Guidance notes to CPR

Although there may be some challenges for the social worker in obtaining views from pre-verbal children or those who are developmentally delayed, it is important that creative ways of obtaining the child's views are used through picture and story books, play, drawing, etc. See Useful Resources for a list of children's books available from BAAF which can be helpful in this work.

You should include views expressed by the child in other settings, e.g. at contact visits with birth parents, in school or nursery, or in the foster home, and include any comments made to others, e.g. foster carers, contact workers, parents. All views should be recorded even where these are contradictory. You can provide the context and analysis of this in the next section.

Be aware that this work may need to be undertaken over a period of time – the following extract shows the importance of this.

CASE STUDY

David (aged 12) remembered initially talking about adoption with his social worker, and did not discuss it with anybody else, not even his foster carers. At first he said he did not understand and asked his social worker many questions.

David: *He had to explain it to me a couple of times and then I had my queries. It took me quite a while. And I kept asking questions all over again and he answered them.*

Interviewer: *Can you remember any of the questions you asked him?*

David: *How long will I be with my mum and dad?...I can't remember what the other questions were.*

Although David could not recall what else he wanted to know at this stage, he was positive about this social work support. He said: *He [social worker] kept explaining it to me and he kept asking me if I understood.*[1]

It will be important to update this section before a match is considered, as the child's views may change when he/she starts to understand the plan for adoption and realise that he/she is not returning to their parents or extended family and contact arrangements are reduced.

Social worker's analysis of the child's views

Social worker's summary of the wishes and feelings of the child

This should include an assessment of the child's level of understanding and give details of any direct work undertaken.

Guidance notes to CPR

- Set out what work/discussion has taken place with the child in order to obtain his/her views and who has been involved with this, e.g. social worker, social work assistant, foster carer.

- What is the child's level of understanding about what adoption means?

- What does the child understand about his/her current situation and future plans for him/her?

- Are the child's wishes and feelings being influenced by others, e.g. birth parents, current carers, siblings?

---

[1] Thomas C and Beckford V with Lowe N and Murch M (1999) *Adopted Children Speaking*, London: BAAF, p 26

- Give context to the child's views and expressed preferences – is he/she seeking to replicate his/her birth family experience or current care situation?

- Have the child's views changed over time?

Information about the child's parents and other significant people

This section should be shared with the parent. Each parent should be given the opportunity to comment on the accuracy of the information included about them in the report.

- **Set out how the birth father acquired PR, e.g. by marriage to the birth mother, registration on the birth certificate (after 1 December 2003), a parental responsibility agreement with the birth mother or a parental responsibility order.**

- **If there are any issues relating to the birth parents' immigration status, state whether legal advice has been sought and set out advice received.**

- **Relevant information should be summarised for this section. This will include the parents' own experience of being parented, patterns of relationships and any care history.**

- **Care should be taken when naming individuals, for example, mother's former partners, where these have no relationship to this child. First names or initials should be used where necessary.**

- **Where information is not available, state why not and the efforts made to obtain it.**

- **This section should include the birth of any other children of this parent. It should highlight significant events and dates where known but not duplicate detailed information from elsewhere in the report.**

- **There will be a need to update information in this section where additional information becomes available after the initial completion of this report, e.g. following care and placement order proceedings or after birth parent counselling.**

Guidance notes to CPR

Information for this section should hopefully come from the birth parents but can also be obtained from the current or previous case files, court reports, parenting assessments and other professionals who know or have worked with the birth parents, e.g. independent birth parent counsellors, family support workers or contact supervisors.

Where a birth mother has refused to give full details of the birth father, see if she would be prepared to give "soft information" about him such as a description, likes, dislikes or interests, as these will be helpful for a child/adopted adult later on.

When completing the descriptive sections on birth parents, keep in mind what details a child or young person would like to know.

> ...information about my mum – my tummy mum – what she looks like, what's her name, mad things like that...I think you need more info about why your tummy mummy and daddy couldn't handle you and just give up...I want to know more of what the social workers know but my mummy doesn't.[2]

You should include the following details.

- Descriptions of their **physical features** such as their hair colour, including natural hair colour, colour of their eyes, complexion and skin tone.

- Encourage birth parents to describe themselves and include their **self-descriptions**.

- Do they wear glasses or have any **distinguishing marks** including piercings or tattoos?

- Describe their **stature**, especially where they are above or below average e.g. height, weight.

- Do they have any preference for **how they dress**; particular types of clothing or fashion?

- When describing the birth parent's **personality,** try not to use only negative traits – try to find positive ones. You can use the parent's own description where available or find out how they are described by other relatives and friends. Remember that the way in which they relate to you or other social workers is not necessarily indicative of how other people experience them.

- Set out their **interests**, e.g. favourite TV programmes, football teams, likes and dislikes, meeting friends, type of music, etc.

- Give brief details of their **education** – where they went to school, at what age they left school. Did they achieve any qualifications or awards? What is/was their favourite subject at school? Did they have a positive relationship with any teachers?

- Give details of any current or previous **employment**, including comments where available about the birth parent's attitude to and availability for work.

- Describe their **home**, for example, type of accommodation, how long they have lived there, how well the home is maintained, and give some information about the **neighbourhood** and area in which they live, e.g. is it an area of high deprivation, how involved are they with their neighbours and local community activities, what are the meeting places in the area – pubs, community centres, etc?

- Where the parent has not given consent to their **health** information being shared or has not completed the adoption health reports, try to obtain some information about relevant health issues of all known extended family members that may have

---

[2] Harris P (ed) (2008) *The Colours in Me*, London: BAAF, pp 95–96.

implications for the child, particularly those with a known genetic relevance. Be aware of "self-reported" information or self-diagnosis and clearly set this out as such.

- Where describing **emotional health**, try to be specific about classification or diagnosis, e.g. depression, personality disorders. Where possible, give relevant context, e.g. impact of substance misuse, lifestyle, early childhood experiences.

- When completing the **summary and brief social history**, you may refer to other chronologies but do not "cut and paste" long, detailed chronologies setting out all previous contacts.

- Do not include **third-party information** that should not be shared, e.g. stillbirths, terminations, information relating to other family members and not relevant to the child's adoption.

- Provide a **brief summary** of the birth parent's own childhood experience and include details of all known children, even if living with another parent.

An example is provided in Appendix E.

The child's siblings

Siblings and half-siblings

Every sibling and half-sibling listed on the family tree/structure should be included. Where information is incomplete, state why and the efforts taken to obtain it.

Surnames should be withheld where necessary (e.g. where the child is adopted) and birth names, not adopted names, should be used.

Where the child is placed elsewhere, e.g. previously adopted, relevant information may be sourced from previous case files or current post-adoption support teams. Include the outcome of sibling assessments, and where a decision has been made to place children separately, give clear reasons for the decision so that the adopters and the child can understand why the decision was made.

Guidance notes to CPR

The importance of a child's siblings is enshrined in legislation and reflected in research findings and the testimonies of birth and adopted children and adopted adults. It is recognised as likely to be the longest relationship the child will have in their lives.

In 2014 a new regulation – 12A(2) of the Adoption Agencies Regulations 2005 – was introduced, which requires the agency, 'where it is considering adoption for two or more siblings, to consider whether they should be placed separately or together'.

SG Chapter 3 sets out that:

There should be a clear decision-making process which enables social workers to decide early whether it is in the best interests of each child to be placed together or separately, and the impact on each child of that decision. The decision-making process should be set out clearly with the supporting information and evidence so that all the professionals who are involved in making decisions about each child's future can see how and why the decision was reached. It will also be important in future for the child, as an adult, to be able to see how and why a decision was reached. The decision should be based on a balanced assessment of the individual needs of each child in the group, and the likely or possible consequences of each option on each child.

SG Chapter 5 sets out that:

Where siblings cannot be placed together with the same family, it is important to ensure that contact arrangements between them are given very careful attention and plans for maintaining contact are robust. Contact arrangements may need to be varied as the children's relationships and need for contact change over time.

The following points should be considered.

- When completing information on the child's siblings, make all efforts to include up-to-date information, as this will be important for both the child and the adopters in the future.

- Ensure that information is included on both maternal and paternal siblings and half-siblings of the child.

- Describe the siblings' temperaments and interests – if information is being taken from old case files, give the date of that information.

- Information gathered for a sibling assessment from various people involved with the siblings – foster carers, contact supervisors, nursery staff or teachers – can provide information on the nature of the sibling relationship.

- It is important to include what is known about the sibling relationships prior to the children coming into care and how these have changed.

- Do not "cut and paste" information between reports on different siblings in the family – rather, ensure that each comment is relevant to the specific relationship between the child and this sibling.

Other significant relatives or relevant people

Other significant people may include step-parents/ grandparents/other relatives who have had care of the child

Anyone who holds parental responsibility should be included. Whether an individual is "significant" should be assessed on a case-by-case basis, seeking input from the child through direct work, using ecomaps or genograms where appropriate.

Set out how the parental responsibility has been obtained, i.e. through a residence order, special guardianship order, parental responsibility agreement entered into by a step-parent with a birth parent, parental responsibility order to step-parent, or being appointed as a legal guardian after a parent's death.

Guidance notes to CPR

This section should include and be linked to people featured on the family tree/genogram and also to section 30, in which you explore why the child cannot be placed within his/ her birth family or with other connected persons.

Part 2:
Contact arrangements

2

The section on current contact needs to set out not just the detail of how and when contact takes place but also to describe what level of engagement takes place between the child and their relative and how the current contact is seen to be meeting the child's needs.

You could include the following information.

- Who else is involved in the contacts that take place?

- What is the child like before and after contact?

- What interaction is seen between the child and his/her relative?

- How does the child benefit from the contact?

- Is any work done to improve the quality of contact?

Proposed contact arrangements

This should reflect the care plan and include consideration of the likelihood of any existing relationship continuing and the value to the child of it doing so.

Include the proposals for any reduction in contact between the final hearing and match. Any changes to the contact plan made after the CPR is first written, e.g. at the point of the care order or placement order, should be included.

The support plan should detail how contact plans are to be supported. Further information can be found in Statutory Adoption Guidance, Chapter 5, on contact.

Guidance notes to CPR

- When completing the section on future contact, the views of the child and their siblings, any expert witnesses and those involved in the sibling assessment should be considered.

- There should be discussion with the social worker or team who would be involved in facilitating or supervising such contact, e.g. the letterbox co-ordinator, adoption support team or contact centre, to ensure that proposed plans can be supported.

- The frequency of any forms of contact should be determined by the needs of the child, rather than those of his/her adult relatives, but research has shown that active engagement with adoption support workers can ensure that contact is a positive experience for both parties.

- Where there is going to be indirect contact between siblings, thought needs to be given to how this can be child-friendly, perhaps through involving the use of DVDs, Skype, email, etc.

Part 3:
Summary of the actions of the adoption agency

3

Chronology of the key decisions and actions taken by the agency in respect of the child

> **The chronology of decisions and actions taken by the agency relates to key decisions and actions in relation to the adoption plan**
>
> **This should include dates of key review decisions, care planning meetings, family group conferences and professional meetings where the adoption plan was progressed, rather than every meeting or contact. Important decisions, such as to place siblings together or apart, considering or ruling out family members or foster carers wishing to adopt, should be recorded.**
>
> **Dates of notifications sent to birth parents and when independent support was offered should also be included.**
>
> **Guidance notes to CPR**

When completing this chronology, remember that it is not a duplicate of the chronology prepared for court and does not need to include all actions, e.g. visits, telephone calls.

Start the chronology from the local authority's first involvement with the birth parents in relation to *this* child – whether that was a referral, meeting or decision to accommodate.

Do not use acronyms as these will not mean anything to readers such as the child, adopted adult or adopters in the future.

Where a Fostering for Adoption placement has been made under Regulation 25(a), include the date of the decision for temporary approval.

There is an example of a chronology and the key decisions to include in Appendix F.

Support to birth parents and their views

> **Wherever possible, and if the agency considers it appropriate, this record [birth parent's views] should be completed by the birth mother or father in their own words. It may be used as an important source of information for the agency in making its decisions and, when and where appropriate, for the child and the adoptive parents in understanding the child's background.**
>
> **It is important that the birth mother and father understand the importance of these questions and the reasons why they are being asked. The form should be used wherever possible within the context of a counselling interview(s) (required in Regulation 14, AA Regulations 2005).**
>
> **This section of the form could be revisited and updated at later points after the care proceedings, before matching or the adoption order application if the birth parents have been helped to make further contributions or changed their views. The information from the forms will be included in the main report and a copy of the forms placed on the child's adoption file.**
>
> **Guidance notes to CPR**

As stated previously, legislation requires that birth parents should be able to comment on what is written about them in the CPR but also encouraged to give their views and wishes about the plan for their child to be adopted.

Even when they are not agreeing to adoption, birth parents can be supported to give their views on what they want for their child in the future. Where writing is not their preferred means of communication, they could be assisted to express their wishes by their social worker or independent birth parent support worker.

National Minimum Standards (NMS) also set out these expectations.

> *NMS 12.5: The wishes and feelings of the birth parents, siblings and other members of the birth family, and other people the agency considers relevant, are listened to and are valued and respected. They are taken into account when making decisions. Where they are not acted upon, the reasons for not doing so are explained to the individual so that they understand why their views are not reflected in their child's care. The wishes and feelings and, if applicable, the reasons why they are not being acted upon, are recorded on the child's case record and included in the Child's Permanence Report.*
>
> *NMS 12.7: Birth parents are given the opportunity to comment on what is written about them or their circumstances before the information is passed to the adoption panel or to the child's proposed adoptive parents.*

Where birth parents are not willing to engage with the child's social worker, efforts should be made to obtain their views through other professionals working with them or through their legal representatives who can help them to understand the importance of this for the child later on.

If the birth parents are reluctant to give their views whilst the court proceedings are ongoing, it may be possible to go back to them at a later stage before the match to give them a further opportunity to respond.

Ability and willingness of family members or relevant persons to care for the child

> **Complete a separate sheet for each individual who has been approached or who has approached the agency with a view to offering a permanent placement for the child. Assessments of family members will be available to the court as part of the evidence submitted. This section does not need to replicate these assessments but should provide a brief summary of the analysis and conclusions.**
>
> **Guidance notes to CPR**

This section is a significant part of your evidence as to why the child cannot be placed with either his/her birth parents or extended family members. For the child and prospective adopters who will not necessarily see the full assessments on family members that are submitted to the court, this will help them understand why family members were not suitable.

Ensure that there are clear reasons set out for each assessment of the birth parent or family member – a general comment that the recommendation was negative will not provide understanding for the child in the future of why each person was not considered able to care for him/her.

Following a summary of the assessment and its outcome, it is helpful to give an indication of how the family member has responded to the outcome of the assessment and what role they could play in the child's life in the future, i.e. providing information for life story work, or maintaining some form of contact with the child where this is seen to be in the child's best interests.

Summary of the reasons for considering that adoption would be in the child's best interests

> **Where the reasons for considering that adoption would be in the best interests of the child relies, in part, on expert opinion, the outcome of the assessment should be summarised. The full reports should be available to the agency decision-maker but will only be available to the prospective adopters with leave of the court.**
>
> **Social workers should be aware of the need to be compliant with the ruling in _re BS_ and use the information gathered and analysed in the social work care template shown below to inform the report.**
>
> **Guidance notes to CPR**

SG Chapter 1 states that:

> _The CPR must contain an analysis of the options that have been considered by the agency for the future care of the child, and explain why adoption is considered the preferred option._

SG Chapter 1 sets out that:

> _The social worker will need to think carefully about which documents should be sent to the adoption panel or decision-maker. It is unhelpful to them to receive hundreds of pages through which they have to sift to find the important information, so a summary of the information, agreed by all parties, should be provided to them. The full reports must, however, be available to them._

Any viability or parenting assessments should be made available for the agency decision-maker when making their decision in case they are needed.

- Following the recent case law in _Re BS [2013] EWCA Civ 1146_, social workers must ensure that they address _all_ the care options which are realistically possible and provide analysis of the arguments for and against each option so that they can demonstrate why they have concluded that adoption is the right plan. A Table of Realistic Placement Options offers a format on which these arguments can be clearly recorded.

- Where there is likely to be some challenge about whether adoption is a realistic plan, e.g. where siblings are being separated, or for older children, disabled children or children with complex needs, there should be particular thought and careful analysis, which can be supported as appropriate by relevant research.

(a) The relative merits of a placement order and other orders (such as a residence order or special guardianship order), including an assessment of why the child's long-term interests are likely to be best met by adoption rather than by any other order

In this section, the focus is only on the arguments for or against specific orders, rather than all placement options.

(b) Recommendations as to whether there should be future contact arrangements (or not), including whether a contact order under section 26 of the 2002 Act should be made

This will be a summary of the arrangements set out in Part 2. Social workers should be mindful of the welfare checklist requirement and show that they have considered the benefit for the child of continuing a relationship with the people who are significant to him/her and how this could be achieved. They should be aware of NMS 8.2, which states that:

> Where siblings cannot be placed together with the same prospective adopters or adopters, contact arrangements with other siblings are made when it is in the best interests of each of the children.

The Children and Families Act 2014 introduced a new section 51(3) to the ACA 2002. This enables the court, before making an adoption order, to consider whether there should be any order made about contact arrangements. The court is able, on its own initiative or following an application from the adoptive parents, the child, or anyone who has obtained the court's leave to make an application, to make either a contact order or an order prohibiting contact between the child and a named person or people.

Whilst it is anticipated that most contact, whether direct or indirect, will be by voluntary arrangement, there should be consideration of whether such an order may be needed, particularly whether a no contact order is needed to safeguard the child and his/her adoptive family.

Examples of family trees/ genograms and a family structure

Maternal family tree/genogram

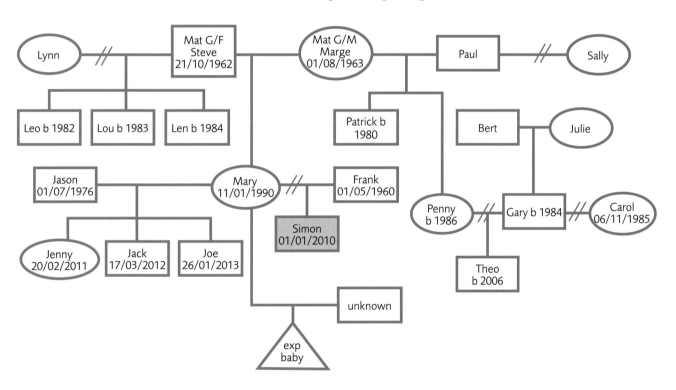

Paternal family tree/genogram

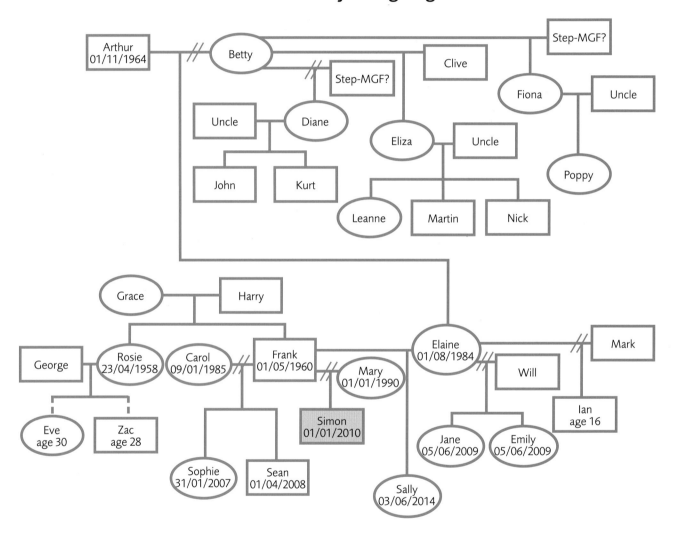

Family structure

Subject Simon 01/01/2010

Mother Mary 11/01/1990
Jason 01/07/1976 – mother's partner/ex-step-father, currently in prison
Jenny, half-sister 20/02/2011 – child of mother and Jason
Jack, half-brother 17/03/2012 – child of mother and Jason
Joe, half-brother 26/01/2013 – child of mother and Jason

Expected baby – half-sibling – child of mother and unnamed father

Steve 21/10/1962 – maternal grandfather
Marge 01/08/1963 – maternal grandmother

Leo, Lou and Len, uncles – mother's half-brothers
Patrick, uncle – mother's half-brother
Penny, aunt – mother's half-sister*
Gary – Penny's former partner (Gary previously in a relationship with Frank's ex-partner)
Theo, cousin b 2006 – child of Penny and Gary

Father Frank 01/05/1960
Elaine 01/08/1984 – step-mother – father's current partner
Jane 05/06/2009 – step-mother's child by Will
Emily 05/06/2009 – step-mother's child by Will
Ian, step-mother's child by Mark
Sally 03/06/2014 – half-sister, child of father and step-mother
Arthur 01/11/1964 – step-mother's father*

All highlighted above live in the same household

Carol 09/01/1985 – father's previous partner*
Sophie 31/01/2007 – half-sister, child of father and Carol
Sean 01/04/2008 – half-brother, child of father and Carol

Grace, paternal grandmother
Harry, paternal grandfather
Rosie, paternal aunt
George, paternal aunt's partner
Eve, cousin age 30*
Zac, cousin age 28*

The above family structure is written to accompany the two genograms. The child who is the subject in this case was living in the father's household prior to coming into care. He therefore had a relationship with all members of that family. His step-mother's father was assessed as a potential carer and is therefore included as a significant person.

The father's previous partner, mother of two half-siblings, is another significant person, also assessed as a potential carer.

The mother is expecting another child who will be a maternal half-sibling and who is known not to be the child of her current partner. It is possible that this child's plan will be adoption. This baby may be placed with the subject.

* indicates family members who were subject to viability assessments.

APPENDIX B: Views of Children's Guardian for Child's Permanence Report (CPR)

Name of child:
....

Name of social worker:
....

As social worker for the above named child, I am proposing to recommend that this child should be placed for adoption. SGSG 2.68 states that 'Where court proceedings are taking place, it is important that the Children's Guardian's views are conveyed to the decision-maker, particularly if these differ from those of the local authority'.

In order to assist the agency decision-maker in reaching their decision, it would be helpful to know your provisional view on the proposed plan of adoption for this child based on the information available to you at this time.

Your view and reasons:
....

....

....

....

....

Name of Children's Guardian:
....

Signature:
....

Date:
....

Thank you for completing this form.

APPENDIX C:
Example of child's chronology of care

Age of child (yrs and mths)	From	To	Placement details – name of parent/carer and observations on the care provided	Reason for move
	02/11/2012	03/11/2012	David was born at 2.41am at Heartlands Hospital. His delivery was normal. His mother, Jane Brown, says that she only smoked cannabis on very rare occasions during her pregnancy. David did not suffer from neonatal abstinence or any other difficulties. Jane was observed to be loving and caring for David, feeding and changing him without prompting. Nurses stated that they had no concerns regarding her care of David.	Discharged from hospital
1 day–5 months	03/11/2012	30/03/2013	David was discharged from hospital and lived with his mother and his half-sister, Alice, at the family address: Flat 1, Old Oak Road, Castle Wood, Birmingham B76 9HH. A pre-birth conference had been held on 18 October where David (unborn child) was made subject to a child protection plan under the category of neglect. The significant concerns were substantial drug use by both Jane and her partner (David's father), Jamie Smith, as well as ongoing evidence of domestic violence. Throughout this care period, Jane admitted that there were times when she found caring for the children more difficult. David was often left in his cot without stimulation and the health visitor noted nappy rash on a couple of occassions due to him being left in a nappy for too long. Jane says David never cried and was happy in his cot. Care was described as inconsistent and chaotic.	Went to live with grandparents as mother felt unable to cope

5 months	30/03/2013	05/04/2013	David lived with his maternal grandfather, Alan Brown, and his wife in Northamptonshire. Initially, Alan looked after David at David's mother's request without the knowledge of children's services, but he was then contacted on 2 April by children's services to ascertain if he would be able to care for David for a short period of time whilst a further assessment of Jane's drugs misuse was undertaken. Alan said he would only look after David until 5 April 2013 as they were due to go on holiday abroad. Both Alan and his wife cared adequately for David throughout this period. He was fed and changed regularly and did not spend all his time in his cot. They bought a bouncing seat for him and he appears to have had more interaction with others. He was described as undemanding and easy to care for. Although visitors were a regular feature, it was a calmer environment and the quality of care David received was described as consistent.	Grandparents going on holiday but didn't wish to care for young child long term
5 months	05/04/2013	26/04/2013	David went to live with his maternal aunt, Sarah Brown, and her family. However, on 26 April 2013, during an unannounced home visit to Sarah Brown's address, it was observed that Gary Jones was present and that David had been left in the care of his mother, in spite of a Working Agreement stipulating that no unsupervised contact should take place between David and Jane and that David should have no contact with Gary Jones, as he posed a risk to children. The quality of care David received here was similar to that when he was living with Jane. It was a noisy, busy house and the quality of care was inconsistent. With three other small children in the house, Sarah says she did the best she could but 'couldn't be spending all my time with him'. It appears he again was left either in a cot or a baby bouncer for most of the time. Often Sarah's seven-year-old daughter would be responsible for giving David his bottle while he was propped up in a chair.	David admitted to care due to concerns regarding care being given by maternal aunt
5–8 months	26/04/2013	12/07/2013	David was accommodated on 26 April 2013 under section 20 of the Children Act 1989, and placed in local authority foster care. Concerns remained in respect of Jane's ability to meet David's basic care needs and keep him safe, and further concerns that Sarah Brown had breached the Working Agreement. David was placed in the care of his current foster carers, Andrew and Karen Pollock. Andrew and Karen described David as quiet and withdrawn when he arrived. He rarely cried: 'It's as if he doesn't expect anyone to come to him'. This was a loving and stimulating environment in which all David's needs were both promoted and met.	Foster carers needed to go to Ireland at short notice for brief period. Not appropriate to take David.

8 months	12/07/2013	15/07/2013	David went to Richard and Susan Clarke, local authority-approved foster carers, for three days while Andrew and Karen Pollock went to Ireland to visit a relative who was terminally ill. Richard and Susan are also friends of Andrew and Karen so have met David prior to the respite period. Susan spent a day with him prior to the move and did most of the caring for him on that day and for the three days David was with them. David did not sleep particularly well the first night and seemed to "miss" Andrew and Karen.	Returned to Andrew and Karen Pollock
8 months	16/07/2013	To present	David returned to live with Andrew and Karen Pollock. He continues to progress well in a warm and nurturing environment. He is now meeting all his developmental milestones and is more engaging. See foster carer's report.	

Health information collected by BAAF forms

Consent form

To be completed by the birth parent or the child/young person with capacity to consent, or another adult with parental responsibility or representative of local authority if local authority has parental responsibility.

- To obtain consent from the birth parent to access their health history from various sources.

- To obtain consent to access comprehensive health history of the child/young person from relevant sources.

- To obtain consent to allow the agency to share health information with health professionals and others involved in provision of health care and planning.

- To obtain consent to allow the agency to share relevant health information with current and future carers.

- To allow the child or young person to receive relevant health information at suitable times in the future.

- To accompany Forms M/B, PH, IHA-C, IHA-YP, RHA-C and RHA-YP to access information held by physicians and their records, and permit the sharing of health information.

Form M: Obstetric report on mother

To be completed by doctor or midwife.

- Information on health of mother before, during and after delivery to help placement and planning.

- To enable agencies to pass on relevant information to new GPs and carers.

- To provide information about the birth mother, which will assist in correct interpretation of medical findings when children are older or have reached adulthood.

Form B: Neonatal report on child

To be completed by doctor with access to birth records.

- To provide basic information for current health care and decisions regarding future placements.

- To contribute to written information to adopters for babies, sleeping/feeding patterns.

- To provide information for new GP in accordance with AAR 2005.

- To provide information about the child's earliest days which may be relevant to health care later and will be valued by adopted adults.

Form PH: Health report on birth parent

To be completed by each birth parent with assistance from social worker if required.

- To provide family health history to aid planning.

- Information to contribute to care of child's health.

- To provide an opportunity to discuss with birth parents the health history of their extended families, which will increase genetic knowledge.

- To demonstrate to the child later that their birth parents gave thought and consideration to their future welfare.

- If birth parent is not available, complete with near relative and indicate source of information.

Forms IHA-C (0-9), IHA-YP (10-18): Initial health assessment (child/young person)

To be completed by doctor (or in Wales, a nurse) experienced in paediatrics or adolescent health, and developmental assessment.

- For looked after children and children to be placed for adoption.

- To provide a comprehensive and holistic health assessment to contribute to initial health plan for first review (important for child and to protect carer/agency).

- To provide carers with a picture of the child's current physical and developmental state.

- To be used as a baseline for future health assessments.

Forms RHA-C (0-9), RHA-YP (10-18): Review health assessment (child/young person)

To be completed by a nurse or doctor experienced in paediatrics or adolescent health, developmental assessment and health promotion, or the child's GP or, in the case of children with medical conditions or disabilities, the relevant specialist.

- To provide a comprehensive review of the health and development of looked after children, to determine if previous health care plans have been carried out, to identify new issues and to modify the care plan as needed.

Forms CR-C (0–9) and CR-YP (10–18): Carers' report (child/young person)

To be completed by the carer.

- To provide a description of the child or young person's emotional and behavioural wellbeing in the carer's own words, and to indicate change over time.

- To provide information that will give a clear and realistic picture of the child or young person, to inform care planning, to promote stability in placements and to assist future carers.

Prepared by Florence Merredew, BAAF Health Consultant

APPENDIX E:
Example of birth mother's summary and brief social history

Date	Detail any significant events – carers, place of residence, bereavement or loss, major illness – to give a brief social history of the birth mother relevant to this CPR
20/02/1990	Jane was born at New Street Hospital, Birmingham, to her parents, Alan and Patricia Brown. Jane recalls a negative childhood with her father misusing alcohol, experiencing mental health difficulties and being violent towards her mother. Jane has a sister, Sarah, who is five years older than her.
September 1994	Jane attends Four Dwellings Primary School.
September 2001	Jane attends Four Dwellings Secondary School.
December 2005	Jane's parents separate. Jane and her sister remain with their mother but have frequent contact with their father.
May 2006	Jane finishes secondary education.
May 2006	Jane meets and starts a relationship with DR. The relationship ends when she tells him that she is pregnant.
December 2006	Jane gives birth to daughter, Alice, at New Street Hospital, Birmingham.
February 2011	Jane meets Jamie Smith through Facebook and they begin a relationship. This proves to be a turbulent relationship with many domestic disputes between the couple.
02/11/2012	Jane gives birth to her second child, David.
13/11/2012	Jane returns to live at Flat 1, Old Oak Road, Castle Wood, Birmingham, which is within Galeano Place, run by Friendship Housing. The organisation provides help and support for vulnerable people to enable them to move on to live independently in the community.
January 2013	A number of referrals are made to children's services with regards to Jane and Jamie's turbulent relationship and their anger management issues, as well as their minimal knowledge of child care and development issues.
February 2013	Jane and Jamie decide to end their relationship and Jamie moves out of the family home.
March 2013	Jane appears in court after she is arrested and charged with possession of cannabis and heroin. She sends David to live with her father and Alice to live with her sister as she says she is finding it increasingly difficult to cope.
26/04/2013	Jane provides consent under section 20 of the Children Act 1989 for her children, Alice and David, to be accommodated by the local authority.
13/06/2013	Jane moves out of her flat at Galeano Place to live in private rented accommodation at Flat 2, John Bright Street, Castle Wood, Birmingham.

APPENDIX F: Example of chronology of key decisions and actions of the agency

Date	Key decision/action
July 2011	An anonymous referral was received raising concerns about neglect of the children. Mother pregnant with third child (Larry, born August 2011). Matter progressed to referral and an initial assessment was undertaken, which resulted in no further action being taken. The family was closed to the Children and Young People's Department (CYPD) on 27.08.2011.
September 2011	Concern raised by police about mother's behaviour towards neighbours. Further assessment. Referral closed on 14.09.11. No further action taken.
October 2011	Contact was made by Housing, stating that Police, Education and Housing felt that the children were at risk of emotional harm, and the family was at risk of eviction following a number of complaints by neighbours. Professionals felt that a Common Assessment Framework (CAF) was not appropriate due to non-engagement. The management decision was that there was a recent assessment undertaken and no safeguarding concerns were identified, therefore there was no role for CYPD. No further action was taken.
December 2011	Contact made by ambulance service with regards to mother's mental health. Progressed to referral, and an initial assessment was undertaken.
March 2012	Decision to undertake a core assessment.
May 2012	A network meeting was held. Family support worker to be allocated to family.
May 2012	Family support worker visit. Mother threatening to kill the children unless they were removed from her care. Mother also making threats to kill neighbours and family support worker. Following discussions with service manager, it was decided that an emergency protection order and section 20 applications were to be made with regard to the children. Mother arrested and served the EPO whilst in custody. Children moved to foster carers. Larry and his siblings were subsequently made subjects of interim care orders.
June 2012	LAC review twin-track while assessments completed.

August 2012	Eldest sibling was moved to an alternative placement due to concerns that his behaviour was very volatile towards his siblings.
September 2012	LAC review continue twin-track while assessments completed.
January 2013	Outcome of psychiatric assessment that mother could not currently safely parent any of the children.
Feb/Mar 2013	Viability assessments of extended family were completed with negative outcomes in regard to those willing to care for Larry and his brother, but eldest sibling could safely be placed with uncle.
Feb/Mar 2013	Outcome of sibling assessment was that Larry should be placed with his brother but that eldest child should be placed separately.
April 2013	Permanency planning meeting. Adoption preferred plan for Larry and his brother. Eldest child to be placed with uncle on a fostering basis with a view to special guardianship order in the future.
May 2013	LAC review confirmed plan of adoption.
June 2013	Agency decision that Larry should be placed for adoption.
August 2013	Larry made subject of a care order and placement order.

List of key decisions to be included in chronology

- Child protection conferences
- Decision to apply for emergency protection order
- Gateway meeting – decision to enter into Public Law Outline process
- Gateway meeting – decision to initiate care proceedings
- Care planning meeting
- Agency decision to place under regulation 25A of Care Planning, Placement and Case Review (England) Regulations 2010 (Fostering for Adoption)
- Permanency planning meeting
- Looked after child (LAC) review
- Note dates and reasons for any plan to place siblings together or apart
- Key decisions relating to contact plans
- Date of adoption panel (relinquished children)
- Date of agency decision
- Dates of and reasons for any changes to plan

Child's Permanence Report checklist

This checklist has been adapted from a document used by Dudley Metropolitan Borough Council. Reproduced with kind permission.

Purpose	
1	To give the child the fullest possible account of their history and the circumstances which led to them leaving their birth family and being placed for adoption.
2	To give the adoption panel and the agency decision-maker all the information necessary to make a recommendation and decision that the child should be adopted.
3	To give prospective adopters information about a child that enables them to make an informed decision about whether they can meet a child's needs.
Is the CPR:	
1	Well written and well presented?
2	Are all sections of the report completed fully and accurately?
3	Is the required information recorded in the appropriate section (always refer to CPR guidance notes)?
4	Does the report contain as much history as possible and, where information is missing, are the efforts made to obtain the information fully stated?
5	Does Section 8 contain full information about the child's physical and psychological health, including genetic and hereditary factors? Is the source of the information clearly stated and distinction made between fact and opinion?
6	Does Section 7 record full details of all the child's placements and carers from birth?
7	Does the report contain an unbroken narrative of the child's history starting before birth?
8	Does the family history include a balanced but sensitive and honest account of the child's birth parents' history?
9	Does the report include a full assessment of the child's needs, including any special needs relating to culture, ethnicity and disability?
10	Does the report make the child come alive?

11	Is the planning process clearly outlined? Is what happened and why clearly explained, including why adoption is the best way of meeting the child's need for permanence?
12	Are the views of the child's birth parents, carers, Children's Guardian and independent experts clearly recorded?
13	Is a full and accurate chronology of the agency's actions included?
14	Is an accurate family tree/genogram attached?
15	Are significant details included? These should include: ● child's birth weight ● details of birth ● why the child's name was chosen ● physical description of the child and his/her birth parents
16	Is there evidence of clearly thought out plans for placement, with clear explanations of plans for contact, placement of siblings together or apart?
17	Are reports from the child's foster carer, school, nursery and any other significant sources attached?
18	Are details of siblings included in the appropriate section?
19	Does the report conclude with a full summary that brings together an analysis of all available information supporting the plan for adoption?
20	Is the report signed by the social worker, manager, child (if appropriate) and birth parents? If the child's parents have not seen or signed the report, reasons should be given.

Agreement form

Agreement form for information held on a child's file to be shared with adopted adult when a request for access to information is received once they are over 18

Name of person:

....

Address:

....

Telephone numbers:

....

Email address:

....

Relationship to the adopted person:

....

(This could be, for example, an aunt, uncle, cousin, grandparent, family friend, foster carer, teacher)

I understand that (name and date of birth of adopted person), once an adult, may want to access information about his/her background prior to his/her adoption. I have discussed with the adoption worker the range of information that may be requested and the circumstances in which future contact may be made. I therefore agree to the following (please tick the appropriate answer):

I am willing for background information to be given to the adopted person about me and my involvement with and relationship to them

YES   **NO**

I am willing for non-identifying information about me to be passed on to the adopted person

YES   NO

I am willing for my contact details to be given to the adopted person

YES   NO

I want contact to be made with me first by the adoption agency/adoption support agency before I make a decision to have my details given to the adopted person

YES   NO

I am willing to be contacted by the adopted person

YES   NO

I am willing to be contacted by the adoption agency/adoption support agency on behalf of the adopted person

YES   NO

Signed: Date:

Witnessed by (insert title, e.g. adoption worker):

Address:

Signed: Date:

Prepared by Julia Feast, BAAF Policy, Research and Development Consultant

Useful resources

Books for use with children in ascertaining their wishes and feelings

Argent H (2007) *Josh and Jaz have Three Mums*, London: BAAF
This story helps to explain the diversity and "difference" of family groups, and encourages an understanding and appreciation of same-sex parents.

Argent H (2012) *Moving Pictures*, London: BAAF
Designed for social workers and carers undertaking direct work with children aged four and above, this book contains a CD-ROM of line drawings designed to spark discussions about moving and permanence.

Bagnall S (2008) *The Teazles' Baby Bunny*, London: BAAF
This simple book for young children provides a gentle introduction to broaching the subject of adoption.

Bell M (2008) *Elfa and the Box of Memories*, London: BAAF
This story looks at the importance of memories, both good and bad, and how they help us to remember the story of our lives.

Daniels R (2009) *Finding a Family for Tommy*, London: BAAF
This story introduces young children, between the ages of 18 months and five years, to the idea of different families and the concept of belonging.

Edwards B (2010) *The Most Precious Present in the World*, London: BAAF
This story looks at themes of loss, separation and belonging, and explains that it is alright to have mixed feelings about adoption.

Foxon J (2003) *Nutmeg gets Adopted*, London: BAAF
The first title in the six-book Nutmeg series, which follows Nutmeg the squirrel's adoption journey.

Foxon J (2007) *Spark Learns to Fly*, London: BAAF
This story looks at the difficult issue of domestic violence and what this could mean for the children involved.

Griffiths J (2007) *Picnic in the Park*, London: BAAF
This colourful book introduces young children to varied contemporary family structures.

Kahn H (2002) *Tia's Wishes*, London: BAAF

Kahn H (2003) *Tyler's Wishes*, London: BAAF

These two story books – one for girls and one for boys – encourage young children to voice their fantasies about adoption and to come to terms with reality. They can be used well before a new family is identified to help explore fears about separation from foster families.

Merchant E (2010) *Dad David, Baba Chris and Me*, London: BAAF
This story helps to explain the diversity and "difference" of family groups, and encourages an understanding and appreciation of same-sex parents.

Pitcher D (2008) *Where is Poppy's Panda?*, London: BAAF
This story explores transition, loss, change and the importance of maintaining continuity in a child's life.

Sambrooks P (2009) *Dennis Duckling*, London: BAAF
This story, aimed at children aged two to five, tells the story of Dennis and his younger sister, who have to leave their birth family to be looked after by foster carers.

Sambrooks P (2011) *Dennis and the Big Decisions*, London: BAAF
This story, aimed at children aged two to five, describes how decisions are made about where looked after children are to live.

Sambrooks P (2014) *Dennis goes Home*, London: BAAF
This story, aimed at children aged two to five, follows Dennis and his sister as they return home to their birth family.

Seeney J (2007) *Morris and the Bundle of Worries*, London: BAAF
This story explores the importance of sharing worries and thereby learning to cope and manage them.

Seeney J (2012) *A Safe Place for Rufus*, London: BAAF
This story explores the ideas of safety and belonging and how these things, or the lack of them, can affect children.